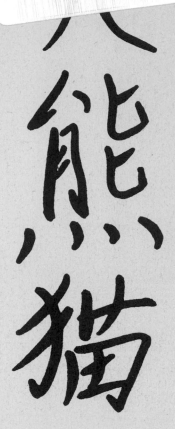

This book is dedicated to Mollie Belov,
who wanted to read about pandas.

In China, giant
pandas are called
giant bear cats.
This is how the
Chinese write ''giant
bear cat.''

ISBN 0-590-31865-9

12 11 10 9 8 7 6 5 4 3 2   2 3 4 5 6 7/8
                              Printed in the U.S.A   07

A BOOK ABOUT

pandas

by RUTH BELOV GROSS

 SCHOLASTIC BOOK SERVICES NEW YORK • TORONTO • LONDON • AUCKLAND • SYDNEY • TOKYO

Far away,
in the mountains of China,
there lives a special kind of animal.
It is called a giant panda.

A full-grown giant panda is as big as a black bear. It is about six feet long from its head to its tail.

Giant pandas are furry and fat.
They look like great big teddy bears,
only they are not brown like teddy bears.
They are black and white.

Their legs are black.
Their shoulders are black.
Their ears are black,
and the fur around their black eyes
is black too.

Everywhere else their fur is white.
Pandas have white faces
and white middles
and short white tails.

In the mountains where the pandas live,
it is cold and damp.
Snow covers the ground until May or June,
and the summers are rainy and wet.

All the year round,
bamboo plants grow tall and thick.

Many years ago, hunters used to go to the
mountains to shoot the pandas.
Then the Chinese government said
that nobody could shoot pandas any more.

Nowadays, Chinese people
sometimes climb the high mountains
to look for a baby panda.
When they find one, they carry it carefully
down the mountains and take it to a zoo.

Scientists have learned about pandas
mostly by watching the pandas that live in zoos.
Every picture in this book was taken in a zoo.

The scientists would like to see how pandas live
in their mountain home in China.
But that is hard to do.

The bamboo plants grow so tall and so thick
where the pandas live that sometimes
all you can see is bamboo.
Sometimes you can hardly push your way
through the bamboo jungle.

It might take weeks to find a panda.
Or you might never find a panda at all.
So there are still a lot of things
we do not know about pandas.

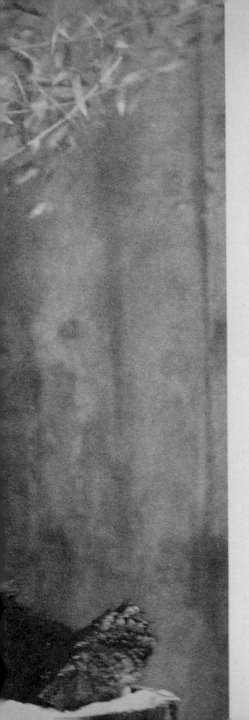

One thing we know about the pandas
in the mountains of China
is what they eat.

They eat the bamboo plants
that grow all around them.
They bite into a bamboo stem
or eat some bamboo leaves
whenever they feel like it.

Pandas in China also eat flowers
and roots and grass. Sometimes they eat
fish and birds and other small animals too.

And once in a while
they take a trip down the mountains
and steal honey from a farmer's bee hive.

Pandas have strong teeth, and they need them for eating bamboo. Some bamboo stems are as hard as wood.

A panda picks up food in its hands almost as easily as a person does. It can do this because it has a special bone growing out of each wrist. The bone works the way your thumb works when you hold something.

In the zoo, pandas get plenty of bamboo to eat.

They also eat other things. Some zoos
give their pandas raw apples and carrots and
sweet potatoes, and pans of slurpy rice.
Other zoos give their pandas a soupy meal
of milk and eggs and ground-up vegetables.

In all the zoos, pandas get vitamins
to keep them strong and healthy.

Different pandas like different things to eat.
Here are some of the things that different pandas
have liked: slices of bread, roast chicken,
baked potatoes, and spaghetti.

All pandas like sweet things, and
sometimes they get honey or jam or a chocolate bar
as a special treat.

Pandas in the zoo
usually go to sleep after they eat.
They spend a lot of time sleeping.

Sometimes they lie on their backs to sleep.

Sometimes they lie on their sides.

Sometimes they sit up.

Sometimes they sleep any old way!

What do zoo pandas do
when they are not eating or sleeping?
They are playing!

They turn somersaults.
They stand on their heads.
They climb ladders.
And they just fool around.

Do pandas in the mountains play too?
They probably do.
Nobody really knows.

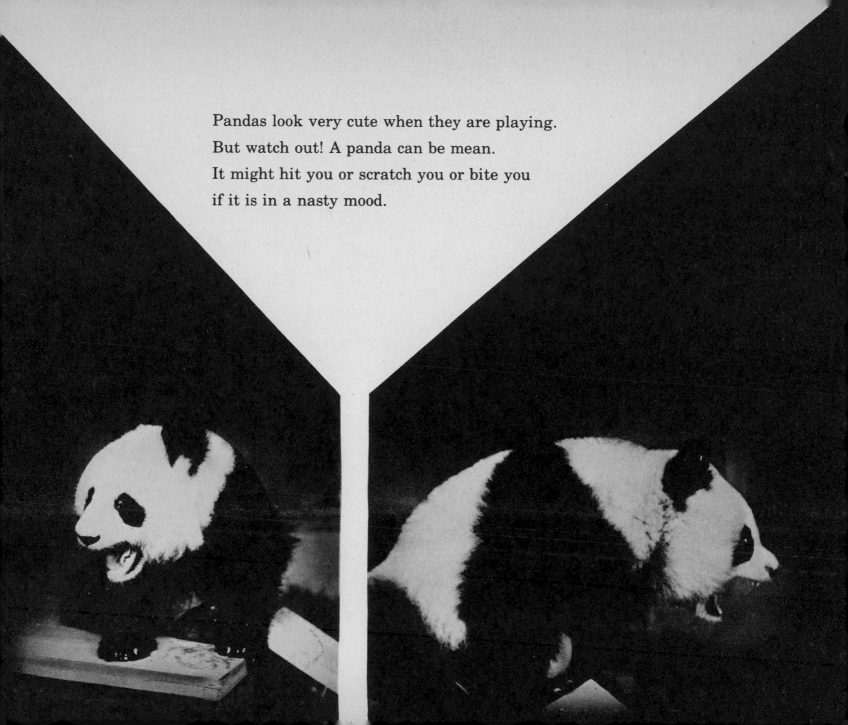

Pandas look very cute when they are playing.
But watch out! A panda can be mean.
It might hit you or scratch you or bite you
if it is in a nasty mood.

The zoo keepers in China
say that female pandas are friendlier
than male pandas.

Other zoo keepers do not agree.
They say that pandas are like people —
every one is different.

Some are growly.
Some are friendly.
Some are sleepy.
Some are bashful.
Some act like clowns.

A brand-new baby panda is very tiny.
It weighs only four or five ounces —
about as much as an apple.

When a panda is born, its eyes are closed.
It has no teeth.
It cannot walk or crawl. It can only roll over.

The mother panda feeds the baby
with her milk. She cuddles it
and holds it close to her body.
She takes care of the baby panda
until the baby panda
can take care of itself.

Pandas do not live together in families.
A baby panda probably leaves its mother
before it is a year old.
Then it lives all alone.

Pandas grow very fast.
By the time a panda is a year old,
it weighs 75 or 80 pounds —
more than a big nine-year-old boy.

By the time a panda is six years old,
it weighs 250 or 300 pounds —
more than a big, fat man.
In the zoo, pandas get weighed
on a special scale.

A full-grown panda is about six feet long.

Pandas can probably mate and have babies
when they are three or four years old.
All the pandas that have mated in zoos, though,
were five or six years old.

So far, ten baby pandas have been born
in zoos. The mother pandas usually had one baby
at a time, but sometimes they had twins.

There are about a dozen zoos in the
whole world that have giant pandas.
Most of these zoos are in China, and that
is where the ten baby pandas were born.

The oldest zoo panda is in his twenties now.
He lives in a zoo in China.
All the other zoo pandas
got sick and died when they were younger.
Scientists think that if a panda stays healthy
it can live as long as 25 or 30 years.

Ling-Ling, who lives in the zoo
in Washington, D.C., cools
off on a hot summer day.

Chi-Chi, the panda who lived in the
London Zoo, liked to take baths. This
is Chi-Chi when she was young,
splashing in her bubble bath.

In some zoos, the pandas have a
pool to cool off in. But most pandas
don't like to go swimming.

Zoo keepers know that pandas come
from a cold, damp place. They want
the pandas to feel at home
in the zoo.

So they give the pandas a cool place
to live. An air-conditioned panda house
is just a little bit warmer
than the inside of your refrigerator.

How do pandas keep themselves clean?

They comb the dirt out of their fur
with their claws.
They lick their fur with their tongues.
And they scratch themselves all over.

A panda can scratch behind its ears.
It can scratch its tail.
It can scratch one foot with another foot.
It can scratch itself just about anywhere.

Scientists have not been able to decide
what kind of animal the giant panda is.

Is it a kind of bear?

Pandas look like bears.
They climb trees and stand on their hind legs
the way bears do.

Pandas do not sound like bears, though.
They sound more like a goat or a lamb bleating.
Sometimes they make soft barking sounds.

Raccoons

A black bear

But scientists know
that you cannot decide
what an animal is just by
looking at it or listening to it.

So the scientists have looked at panda blood
under a microscope. They have measured
panda bones and they have counted panda teeth.
And they still cannot decide what kind
of animal the giant panda is.

Some scientists think that pandas belong
to the bear family.

Some scientists think that pandas are related
to raccoons.

And some say that pandas belong to a *new*
kind of animal family — the panda family.
They say that there are only two members
in this family — giant pandas and red pandas.
(Red pandas are also called lesser pandas.)

Red pandas live in the mountains of China
where the giant pandas live. They are also found
in other mountains to the west.
They eat bamboo and they are good at
climbing trees.

Maybe you have seen a red panda
in a zoo. It has a red coat,
white face, and a
long bushy tail.

A red panda weighs about eight or ten
pounds, and it is about three feet long if
you count its tail. It looks more like a raccoon
than like a giant panda.

There are not many giant pandas left
in the mountains of China—maybe only 500 or so—
and scientists are beginning to worry about them.

There is not as much bamboo as there used to be.
There may not be enough for the pandas to eat.
If there is not enough bamboo, the pandas
could starve to death.

The pandas are not in any other danger.
The Chinese government will not allow people
to hurt them. And they are not likely
to be killed off by other animals.

Once in a while a baby panda might be killed
by leopards or wild dogs,
but a grown panda can take care of itself.

Maybe the pandas will not die out.
Maybe there will be more bamboo soon.
Or maybe the pandas will find other things to eat.

Everyone hopes there will be pandas around
for a long, long time.

■ The author would like to express her appreciation to The New York Public Library for allowing her to use the Frederick Lewis Allen Memorial Room, where this book was written. She would also like to thank members of the staff of the National Zoological Park for their help. And special thanks to Mary Jane Dunton, who designed the book.

The photographs in this book come from the following sources: 2: Ylla/Rapho Guillumette; 4-5: Wide World; 6: Ylla/Rapho Guillumette; 7: Eastfoto; 9: Ylla/Rapho Guillumette; 10-11: Smithsonian Institution; 12: Wide World; 13: Don Carl Steffen, Wide World, Eastfoto, Don Carl Steffen, UPI, Eastfoto; 14: Ylla/Rapho Guillumette; 15: Don Carl Steffen, Pictorial Parade, Michael Lyster/Zoological Society of London; 16: UPI, Granada TV; 17: Ylla/Rapho Guillumette; 18: Alan Band Associates, Koch/Rapho Guillumette, Eastfoto, Ylla/Rapho Guillumette; 19: Koch/Rapho Guillumette, Don Carl Steffen; 20-21: Eastfoto; 22: Fox/Pictorial Parade; 23: Eastfoto; 24: Don Carl Steffen, Fox/Pictorial Parade, Tierbilder Okapia; 25: Fox/Pictorial Parade, Ylla/Rapho Guillumette; 26: Koch/Rapho Guillumette; 27: Eastfoto, Ylla/Rapho Guillumette; 28: Leonard Lee Rue, Leonard Lee Rue/National Audubon Society; 29: UPI; 30-31: Ylla/Rapho Guillumette.

Front cover: Smithsonian Institution. Back cover: Don Carl Steffen.